20th Century

War in the Balkans, as indep
gathered pace, was followed
– and then painful transition to a 'New World Order'.

Fighting for independence

As both Ottoman and Habsburg empires collapsed, nationalist movements spread through the Balkans, adding to the instability of the region. Out of this chaos emerged new states, based on the main ethnic groups. But territorial boundaries were hard to draw and were bitterly fought over. Some areas, such as Bosnia, remained a patchwork of ethnic minorities, as they had done for centuries.

The 'old bridge', Stari Most, across the Neretva river at Mostar has come to symbolise both the best and the worst of the Balkans' multi-ethnic history. Built by the Turks in the 16th century, it was destroyed by Croatian troops in November 1993. Having driven out the Serbs, Croats and Muslims fell to fighting each other for control of the city. Since 1994, an EU administrator, former mayor of Bremen, has been trying to reconcile the two sides.

The Croats made Mostar the capital of their breakaway state, Herceg-Bosna, introducing Croat currency and national emblems. Croat-Muslim hostility and sporadic fighting continued in Mostar even after the Dayton peace accord.

As the 20th century began, nationalism was a rising force throughout the Balkans. While Greece had gained international recognition of its independence in 1832, much of its present territory still remained in foreign hands and its king, George I, was a Bavarian not a Greek. Romania, Serbia and Bulgaria had achieved independence but were unhappy with the extent of their boundaries. Macedonia and Albania were still under Ottoman rule, forming what was left of Turkish-controlled Europe (known as Roumelia).

In 1912 the Balkan League, comprising Bulgaria, Greece, Serbia and Montenegro, was set up to liberate the remainder of the Balkans from Ottoman rule. The League succeeded in driving the Turks from Macedonia and indeed from most of the Balkan peninsula, freeing Albania to become an independent country.

However, the victorious parties could not agree on how to divide Macedonia and, in June 1913, the Second Balkan War broke out when Bulgaria attacked Serb and Greek forces. Fighting Romania and Turkey as well, Bulgaria was soon defeated, leaving Serbia and Greece to divide Macedonia between them, with Bulgaria retaining only a small portion of Pirin Macedonia.

Meanwhile the Habsburg-ruled Croats and Slovenes were trying to win greater autonomy. Support began to grow for a union with the Serbs in a southern Slav state. When the heir to the Austrian throne was murdered in Sarajevo in 1914, Austria declared war on Serbia, taking Europe's conflicting military alliances into World War I.

This turbulent period saw profound changes in Balkan political geography. Between 1913 and 1926 major exchanges of population took place as ethnic groups were accommodated to the new national borders agreed by the great powers.

About 1.3 million Greeks left Turkey (half of them settling in Aegean Macedonia). In addition, about 400,000 Turks left Greece, 25,000 Greeks came from Bulgaria, while over 50,000 Bulgarians left Aegean Macedonia and headed north. The population of northern Greece changed quickly and profoundly. In 1912, for example, Muslims formed over a third of the population. Most had gone by 1939.

The union of southern Slavs came to fruition with the establishment of the Kingdom of the Serbs, Croats and Slovenes in 1918, known after 1929 as Yugoslavia. The powerful Serb army was the foundation of the new country's defence forces, with Serbs retaining their dominant role in the officer corps.

The Kingdom proved an uneasy union. Rivalry grew between 'Catholic' Zagreb and 'Orthodox' Belgrade, with non-Serbs in the Kingdom resentful of Serb power over the government and army. During World War II, a bitter civil war developed. Fascists supported by Hitler took over Croatia and Bosnia under Ante Pavelic, while Tito's partisans fought for a communist state. Atrocities were committed by all sides, with Serb Chetnik irregulars taking revenge for the dreadful carnage wrought by Pavelic's Ustasha terrorists, who slaughtered many thousands of people in some of the worst crimes of World War II.

Nationalism and communism

For Balkan states, the struggles of nation-building that followed independence in the first part of the century gave way to communism after World War II. Only Greece was able to fight off its embrace.

Under communism, ethnic differences were supposed to be downplayed. What mattered were class membership and state control. Throughout the Balkans, literacy, health care and industrialisation programmes were pursued along with brutal repression of dissent.

Today, most Balkan states still have former communists in power, but nationalist thinking again pervades the region, even as it prepares to join the multinational world of free enterprise and global markets.

Greece remained a bastion of freedom in the Balkans – but only just.

Richard Buckley

The Allied victory cemented Tito's own power and a new Yugoslavia was born in which southern Slavs were to be treated as equals in a federal state. Eventually, six Yugoslav 'nations' – Croats, Serbs, Slovenes, Montenegrins, Macedonians and Muslim Slavs – were recognised and given substantial autonomy. Vojvodina and Kosovo became quasi-republics within the federation. Yugoslavia held together for 35 years and seemed to be progressing towards a new kind of multi-ethnic social-market economy.

Tito died in 1980 and, in the following decade, uprisings by Albanians in Kosovo resulted in savage repression by Yugoslav government forces. Nationalism began to breed again as communism declined. The battle for political control of Yugoslavia took place against a background of increasing unemployment in the domestic economy and growing instability in eastern Europe. In this atmosphere, blaming ethnic injustices was an easy route to political power.

Every ethnic group could find grievances – Serbs were too dominant in the army and government, Slovenes and Croats had a better standard of living, and so on. But Serbian nationalists, led by Slobodan Milosevic, took such complaints to new levels of hysteria, conducting a vicious propaganda war against the 'enemies' of the Serbs, i.e., Muslims, Croats and Albanians. Milosevic deliberately poisoned the air, reversing the Titoist policy of Yugoslav 'brotherhood and unity'.

When Soviet communism collapsed, the nationalist cries became louder. International opinion supported the efforts of small nations (such as the Baltic states) to break free from their supposed oppressors. When Slovenia unilaterally declared its independence in 1991, there was outrage at the efforts of Belgrade to quash the rebellion by force, though the West initially backed the preservation of a Yugoslav federation.

Slovenia's successful bid for independence led to the violent unravelling of Yugoslavia, a process which could still engulf the rest of the Balkans if Kosovo, for example, should try to follow Slovenia's example. Kosovo, whose 2 million population is mainly Albanian, has been under Serb military occupation since it lost its autonomy in 1989. Kosovo sits next door to Albania and to a substantial Albanian minority in another newly independent state, Macedonia. Such juxtapositions have been the cause of many past Balkan conflicts.

Over 200,000 people have been killed in the former Yugoslavia and millions of other lives have been ruined by the wars started by extreme nationalists – and then waged by all sides in a dreadful cycle of bloodlust and revenge. The multi-ethnic state of Bosnia is being dismembered, the main beneficiaries being the nationalist governments of Serbia and Croatia. The international community, now busily engaged in 'keeping the peace,' failed to uphold the values of human rights and democracy until they had been almost wiped off the map. Multi-ethnic Yugoslavia can no longer be reconstructed. What chance does the new Bosnian federation have?

Milosevic's government has spent years teaching Serbs to hate Muslims. Now they are expected to work together in a unified Sarajevo. Croats continued to burn down Serb villages while the Dayton talks went on. Even with EU supervision, Mostar* has continued to see bitter conflict between Croats and Muslims. Meanwhile, in Kosovo and Vojvodina, repression continues.

Bosnia is due to hold elections within six to nine months. The hope is that, given a chance to vote freely, the people will choose reconciliation and co-operation. But it seems doubtful whether fair elections are possible in the immediate aftermath of such a brutal war, especially since 60% of the population has been displaced. With local warlords still

What hope for democracy?

Democracy is a new and tender plant in the Balkans. Even Greece, which gave birth to the idea, is a relative newcomer to the practice. Greece's current borders only date to 1913. Surrounded by what it regards as potentially hostile states, Greece remains ultra-sensitive on national security issues. Will the post-Papandreou era produce a more trusting and co-operative approach to Balkan neighbours?

in place, manipulation is all too likely. Moreover, those responsible for ethnic cleansing have not yet been punished. Though the Dayton accord insists that all parties to the agreement must co-operate fully with international investigations of war crimes*, Croatia's President Tudjman promoted Tihomor Blaskic, wanted by the war crimes tribunal in The Hague, to become general inspector of the Croatian Army – hardly a sign of good faith.

Tudjman's dictatorial leanings were further shown during the autumn 1995 elections in Croatia. International observers criticised many aspects of the election, including media bias and the granting of votes and parliamentary seats to Croats living in Bosnia-Herzegovina. In the event, Tudjman's HDZ party won 45% of the total vote, well short of the two-thirds majority he was hoping for – and which would have given him the margin needed to change the constitution and further strengthen his powers. But Zagreb, home to a quarter of Croatia's population, did not vote for the HDZ. Could it be that Tudjman's nationalistic style of politics is on the way out?

Another hopeful sign is the move by Montenegro to distance itself from Serbia, with prime minister Milo Djukanovic travelling overseas to bolster trading and diplomatic links, and stressing Montenegro's desire to join the western free market camp. Romania, Bulgaria and Turkey seem relatively stable. Greece has lifted its boycott of Macedonia*, which itself has avoided military action, despite tensions involving its large Albanian minority. Albania in turn has largely resisted the temptation to stir up trouble in Kosovo and the government in Sofia is no longer claiming that Macedonia is really part of Bulgaria. Hungary has not allowed its dispute with Romania over the Hungarian minority in Transylvania to get out of hand. International pressure and the need for foreign loans and investment should help to strengthen the voices of moderation.

War and sanctions have severely damaged the Balkan economies, with racketeers the only ones to benefit. There is some hope that economic pragmatism will eventually win the day in the Balkans and bring its diverse states into greater co-operation with each other. The opportunities for development are huge, especially with Turkey joining an EU customs union. If Greece can settle its quarrels with its neighbours, all Balkan states will benefit.

Some key dates in 20th century Balkan history

1908 Austria annexes Bosnia-Herzegovina

1912-13 Serbia, Bulgaria and Greece fight Turkey in First Balkan War; disagreement among victors leads to Second Balkan War when Serbia and Greece defeat Bulgaria and divide up most of Macedonia between them; Albania achieves independence

1914 Assassination in Sarajevo of Archduke Ferdinand by the Bosnian Serb, Gavrilo Princip, leads Austria to declare war on Serbia, resulting in First World War

1918-26 Creation of Kingdom of Serbs, Croats and Slovenes (renamed Yugoslavia under its dictatorial King Alexander in 1929); borders re-aligned, following end of World War I; Hungary loses territory to Romania; major exchanges of population between Greece, Bulgaria and Turkey; Montenegro deposes its king and votes for union with Yugoslavia (Bosnia and South Serbia – later Macedonia – were already part of the Kingdom); Kemal Atatürk sets up government in Ankara and works to make Turkey a modern secular state

1939-45 World War II; Pavelic sets up pro-Nazi Ustasha government in Croatia and Bosnia; large-scale massacres of opponents – Serbs, Muslims, Jews; Roma, etc.; Tito eventually gains control of all Yugoslavia and sets up communist government, independent of Moscow; pro-Moscow communists win control of Albania, Bulgaria, Hungary and Romania; Bessarabia (Moldova) is annexed by USSR

1944-49 Savage civil war in Greece; royalists, backed by UK and US, defeat Greek communists based in northern mountains; 50,000 people killed; Yugoslavia expelled from Cominform

1967 Military coup in Greece leads to repressive right-wing rule until democracy is restored in 1974

1980 Death of Tito; leadership of Yugoslavia goes to collective presidency of its six republics

1987 Slobodan Milosevic wins leadership of Serbian League of Communists; he begins press campaign to stir up Serb fears of Catholics and Muslims, and advocates creation of a new 'Greater Serbia'; elected Serbia's President in 1989, he orders harsh repression of dissent by Albanians in Kosovo and removes autonomy from Kosovo and Vojvodina

1989-92 Collapse of Soviet communism leads to Moldovan independence, changes of government and free market reforms in Bulgaria, Romania and Albania, and power struggles in Yugoslavia

1990 In free elections, Franjo Tudjman is elected president of Croatia on a nationalist ticket; Serb-dominated Yugoslav National Army (JNA) confiscates weapons of Croatian and Slovenian defence forces (six months later the Serbs take similar action to disarm Bosnian forces)

1991 Slovenia declares independence; JNA invades but soon withdraws; Croatia declares independence; JNA attacks Croatia; Krajina Serbs declare independence, with capital in Knin; Germany announces recognition of Slovenia and Croatia, pulling EU into formal recognition soon afterwards; international sanctions imposed on rump Yugoslavia (i.e., Serbia and Montenegro)

1992 Bosnian referendum on independence is boycotted by Bosnian Serbs, led by Radovan Karadzic; independence of Bosnia is recognised by EU; ethnic cleansing gets underway in eastern Bosnia, with Muslim villages razed as Serbs take control of Drina Valley; UN sanctions imposed on Serbia; London Conference appoints Lord Owen (who had publicly demanded air strikes on Serb military positions) as mediator; Serbs gain control of 70% of Bosnia and 30% of Croatia; Croatian Bosnians declare 'parastate' of Herceg-Bosna, with capital in Mostar, and begin fighting Bosnian Muslims as well as Serbs; UN provides humanitarian relief but cannot prevent escalation of war

1993-94 UN runs 'safe havens' in Bosnia and Croatia; EU trade and co-operation agreement with Slovenia; EU recognises independence of Macedonia; Nato air strikes on Serbs in eastern Bosnia

1995 Croats retake Knin Krajina and 'ethnically cleanse' it, causing 150,000 Serbs to flee; Croats negotiate return of Eastern Slavonia from Serbs; US mediator Richard Holbrooke persuades Presidents Tudjman, Izetbegovic and Milosevic to sign Dayton peace agreement; EU association agreements become effective for Romania and Bulgaria

1996 Nato troops move in to enforce Dayton agreement (see page 14); the international community's 'High Representative' Carl Bildt begins job of building civil administration in Bosnia

Geography of the Balkans

Steep barren mountains and narrow valleys characterise much of the Balkans, making life hard and communications difficult.

Three distinct features – mountains, valleys and coastal rim archipelago

The word "balkan" is Turkish for mountains. But in modern times the word "balkanisation" has developed a very different meaning – the violent disintegration of countries into smaller ethnic units. Geography plays a part in determining natural borders but people do not fit so easily into clearly defined areas, especially after centuries of invasion, occupation and migration.

Cut off by steep mountains and narrow passes, many Balkan communities have retained a deep suspicion of outsiders. But one advantage of such geography is the potential for using the power of fast-flowing rivers to generate electricity, as shown here at Koman dam in Albania. Hydro-power provides a substantial proportion of electricity in the Balkans (96% in Albania, 49% in Croatia).

Rhodri Jones, Panos Pictures

South-east Europe is a region of great geographical diversity, but can broadly be divided into three types of landscape – mountains, alluvial plains/valleys and coastal archipelago. Greece is a mixture of rugged mountains, valleys and island archipelago, but the pattern is best exemplified by the former Yugoslavia, with its fertile Pannonian plains, steep Dinaric Alps and irregular Adriatic coastline.

Limestone karst is typical in the Dinaric range, and the porous nature of the rock has made surface water precious. Agricultural conditions are often harsh. Most of these mountains remained under Turkish dominion until a hundred years ago and the towns have a more oriental look than those of the northern plains. Slavonia and Vojvodina were under Habsburg rule for centuries and their baroque towns evoke the spirit of Bohemia and Hungary to the north, giving it a distinctively central European feel. The area is relatively well-developed, providing the industrial heartland of the western Balkans as well as its main food-producing region.

Mountain fastnesses are characteristic of Albania, Bosnia, southern Serbia, Macedonia, inland Greece and western Bulgaria. Unlike the Carpathians in Romania, these rugged peaks were untouched by Ice Age glaciers and have narrower valleys than those typical of more northerly ranges. Communications are difficult, and in winter may be next to impossible. In some parts of the Balkans, a tradition of mountain brigandry has flourished over many centuries of occupation and insurgency, with local 'warlords' wielding more effective power than the ruling authorities in remote capitals.

The influence of Italy is still visible in the architecture of the coastal Adriatic towns once ruled by Venice. Here again the dominant rock is limestone and the dry hills are poorly equipped to support agriculture. The spectacularly beautiful coastline, however, has provided the basis for a burgeoning tourist trade since the 1960s, with towns such as Split and Dubrovnik – once the independent city state of Ragusa – attracting many visitors.

The barren coastal mountains have acted as a natural barrier to communications with the interior, causing the Dalmatian coast to develop as a separate entity. This helps to explain the strange horseshoe shape of modern Croatia, which incorporated the narrow coastal strip of Dalmatia after 1920.

The climate of the Balkan region varies from the year-round rainfall, cold winters and warm summers of its northern countries to a Mediterranean pattern of hot dry summers and mild rainy winters. Slovenia exemplifies the first type of climate and Greece the second. Seasonal differences are profound in the mountains, with regular snowfalls and bitter cold affecting many Balkan communities.

Romania, with extensive forest and pastureland, has a typically continental climate, with severe winters. Bulgaria, further south, is milder and has good beaches on the Black Sea coast, with fertile farmland in the Maritsa and Danube valleys. Environmental degradation has severely affected many areas.

This topographical map of the Balkans clearly shows the mountainous nature of the terrain, particularly in its western and southern parts. The Danube forms a key artery in the region and has traditionally been a border between states and even empires. Navigable along most of its length, the Danube (Donau in German) is linked to the waterways of Western Europe, thus connecting the North Sea with the Black Sea. The Danube valley also carries important roads and railways. Other main communication routes follow the river valleys of the Sava, Morava and Vardar rivers through Croatia, Serbia and Macedonia, and the Maritsa river along the borders between Greece, Turkey and Bulgaria. The proposed Via Egnatia, linking Istanbul, Sofia, Skopje and Durrës, could make a big difference to economic development in the region, especially for isolated Albania and landlocked Macedonia. The Greeks are pressing for a north-south road which would run from Greece to Bulgaria and thence across a new Danube bridge into Romania. There are also various projects for oil and gas pipelines linking Russia with the Balkans.

Cultural Diversity

The Balkans are home to three great religions and numerous ethnic groups. The rise of nationalism has divided Southern Slavs into mutually hostile camps.

A complex mixture of Slavs, Albanians, Bulgarians, Romanians, Greeks and Turks – plus other minorities

Among the main ethnic groups in the Balkans, the Southern Slavs are the most numerous. The Slav group includes Croats, Slovenes, Serbs and Montenegrins. Tito's Yugoslavia complicated the picture by defining two other national groups – Muslims (i.e., Slavs who had adopted Islam) and Macedonians, inhabitants of what used to be known as 'South' or 'Old' Serbia.

Shown below is a table showing the approximate ethnic mix of the Balkan countries. The main ethnic groups are themselves divided into disparate communities (e.g., Serbs living in Serbia and those in Bosnia or Croatia). Note that census figures may be affected by political considerations, which encourage the authorities to downplay or exaggerate the presence of minorities. For example, Athens has claimed there are 400,000 Greeks in Albania, while Albania says there are only 60,000.

Ethnic mix of countries

Country	Main group	Minorities
Albania	Albanians 98%	Greeks 2%
Bosnia	Muslims 49%	Serbs 31%, Croats 17%
Bulgaria	Bulgarians 86%	Turks 10%, Roma 3%
Croatia	Croats 78%	Serbs 12%, Bosnians 1%
Greece	Greeks 95%	Macedonians 1%, Turks 1%, Albanians 1%
Hungary	Magyars 98%	Roma 1%
Macedonia (FYROM)	Macedonians 65%	Albanians 22%, Turks 4%
Romania	Romanians 89%	Hungarians 7%, Roma 2%
Slovenia	Slovenes 88%	Croats 3%, Serbs 2%
Turkey	Turks 92%	Kurds 6%
Yugoslavia (Serbia and Montenegro)	Serbs 62%	Albanians 17%, Montenegrins 5%, Yugoslavs 3% Hungarians 3%, Muslims 3%

Cultural diversity is common throughout Europe yet reaches new levels of complexity in the Balkans, because of the interaction of peoples, religions and customs which are inevitable when empires overlap. In addition to the main ethnic groups – Slavs, Albanians, Bulgarians, Romanians, Greeks and Turks – there are various others, including Vlachs (now largely assimilated), Roma ('gypsies'), and substantial minorities of Hungarians, Ukrainians and Slovaks.

Communist Yugoslavia (the name means "the country of the southern Slavs") attempted to solve the problem of ethnic rivalry by stressing the importance of 'brotherhood and unity' and giving separate recognition to 'nations' (those whose homeland was in Yugoslavia) and 'nationalities' (other ethnic minorities living in Yugoslavia). All had freedom to speak their own language and continue their own cultural and religious traditions.

The non-assimilative policy of the Ottomans had allowed ethnic and cultural distinctions to survive. Whereas Islam is an overtly political religion, Christian leaders have usually stressed the separation of church and state. Even so, religion came to be an important distinction between peoples in the Balkans.

Indeed, Yugoslavia decided to recognise a religious grouping as a separate 'nation', though in the context of Yugoslavia, "Muslims" means Slavs who have adopted Islam, rather than Turkish or Albanian Muslims, who were regarded as national minorities. Intermarriage was becoming more and more common before the outbreak of war. Yet only 5% of people in the 1991 census classified themselves as 'Yugoslav' rather than as one of the six 'nations'.

Four separate languages were recognised – Croat, Serb, Slovenian and Macedonian. In fact, Serb and Croat are very similar (though Serb is written in Cyrillic script, Croat in Latin). Slovenian, which uses Latin script, is also similar to Serbo-Croat. Macedonian is closely linked to Bulgarian and both use Cyrillic alphabets. Indeed, the Greeks argue that Macedonian is not really a separate language at all, but an artificial one invented to give credence to the notion of a separate nation of 'Macedonian' Slavs.

Albanian and Romanian are completely separate languages, the one supposedly based on ancient Illyrian, the other on Latin. Most Albanians who profess a religion are Muslim but a third are Christian – despite the many years of atheist rule under the communist dictator Enver Hoxha.

South-east Europe has a reputation for ethnic diversity, but most modern Balkan countries are relatively homogeneous in ethnic terms – though some have significant minorities. In Bosnia, which has long had a 'leopard spot' mixture of ethnic communities, Sarajevo became a renowned centre of multiculturalism and ethnic variety. Before war broke out in 1992, Bosnia's population of some 4.3 million was divided mainly among Muslims (49%), Serbs (31%), and Croats (17%). The rump state of Yugoslavia also has a diverse mix of peoples, though many non-Serbs have left in recent years.

Religion – creating wider divisions than race?

Three religions co-exist in the Balkans, reflecting the historical influence of three great empires – Byzantine (Eastern or Greek Orthodox), Ottoman (Islam) and Habsburg (Roman Catholic).

Mapping out ethnically distinct areas of Bosnia baffled successive teams of peace negotiators until the Dayton accord forced the exhausted combatants to accept an artificial form of partition. Western Bosnia, where Serbs had lived for centuries, was allocated to the Muslim-Croat federation. The traditional Muslim enclaves in and around Srebrenica, scene of a large-scale massacre in the summer of 1995, were given to the Serbs. In both cases, 'ethnic cleansing' has been rewarded with territorial gains. Whether, in the longer term, such divisions can be made to stick remains to be seen.

Large-scale migration has been a feature of Balkan history. In the last few years, more than 700,000 refugees have fled the former Yugoslavia, half of them going to Germany and Austria. (The UK has taken about 8,000.) Altogether, well over three million people have been driven from their homes.

In general, minority rights are not well protected in the Balkans, causing friction between, for example, Greece and Albania, Greece and Turkey, Macedonia and Albania, Bulgaria and Turkey, and Romania and Hungary. Worst off are the Roma 'gypsies'– marked out by their darker skins and a reputation for crime – who are typically at the bottom end of the social scale throughout the Balkans. Racial violence against Roma appears to have increased in recent years.

Religion in the Balkans

Religion plays an important part in the politics of the region. Apart from the historical clash between Islam and Christianity, the Christian church itself is divided into two main traditions – Eastern Orthodoxy and Roman Catholicism. While spiritual leadership of all Roman Catholics rests in the papacy in Rome, the Orthodox church is divided into a number of separate patriarchates, which are often at odds with each other. In early times, there were separate patriarchs for different areas but these were abolished in 1766 when all authority was vested in the Greek Orthodox Patriarchate in Constantinople.

In 1870, under pressure from nationalist movements, the Ottomans, who had always tended to favour Orthodox Christians in preference to the crusading Catholics, agreed to the establishment of a separate Exarchate for the Bulgarian church. This was followed by the creation of the Serbian Orthodox Church in 1879 and the Romanian Orthodox Church in 1885. An autonomous Macedonian Orthodox church was created in 1967, under the rule of Tito's communist government. This was the same year that Albania became the world's first officially designated 'atheist state'.

The Ottomans, under the so called *millet* system, divided people into administrative groups by religion rather than ethnicity. During the centuries of Ottoman rule, many people in the Balkans adopted Islam. However, its adherents have rarely been fanatical. Serb warnings of Muslim fundamentalist activity in the Balkans seem grossly exaggerated.

Religious 'confessions' by country are roughly as follows:

Albania Muslim 65%, Orthodox 20%, Roman Catholic 13%
Bosnia Muslim 40%, Serbian Orthodox 31%, Roman Catholic 15%
Bulgaria Eastern Orthodox 87%, Muslim 13%
Croatia Roman Catholic 78%, Eastern Orthodox 12%
Greece Eastern Orthodox 98%
Hungary Roman Catholic 68%, Protestant 25%
Macedonia *(FYROM)* Eastern Orthodox 67%, Muslim 30%
Romania Romanian Orthodox 87%, Roman Catholic 5%
Slovenia Roman Catholic 84%
Turkey Muslim 99%
Yugoslavia *(Serbia and Montenegro)* Serbian Orthodox 70%, other Christian 10%, Muslim 13%

Understanding
Global Issues

The Troubled Balkans
Tension and conflict in south-east Europe

The Balkan Economies

The Balkans have long been an economic backwater, impoverished by centuries of neglect and mismanagement under both Ottoman and communist rule.

The economic costs of war

In 1990 Yugoslavia was one of the richest countries in the Balkans, with a booming tourist trade and a wide mix of industries which were more accustomed to free market forces than those in most post-communist states. Then came war, hyperinflation, international sanctions and economic chaos.

Less dramatic changes have hit the other Balkan countries but they too are struggling with the dangerous transformation from communism to free market democracy. Poverty and environmental degradation are all too common.

Mountainous terrain in the Balkans has inhibited economic development by making agriculture and the building of trade routes difficult. While the broad northern valleys and various sea ports on the Aegean and Dalmatian coasts enjoyed relative prosperity, most of the Balkans remained largely underdeveloped.

Under the Ottomans, stagnation was encouraged by the fact that non-Muslims, although free to practise their religions and maintain their linguistic and cultural traditions, could not own land and had to pay heavy taxes on trading activities. There was little incentive for entrepreneurship among the Christian population, though many opportunities for advancement for those who converted to Islam.

Subsistence agriculture, carried out by small village communities, remained the norm through much of the Balkans, with sheep and goat herding typical of mountain economies, and the cultivation of olives and vineyards common on lower slopes. In the 20th century, the combination of small landholdings, primitive farming methods, high population growth and lack of economic development eventually led to widespread social unrest.

Communist governments after 1945 tackled these problems through large-scale programmes of collectivisation and industrialisation. Many new roads, rail links and airfields were constructed to ease the long-standing isolation of the Balkans. Illiteracy was greatly reduced and many primitive customs swept

The economies of south-east Europe (UK shown for comparison only)

	Land area (million km²)	*Population*	*Total GDP ($million)*	*GDP per head ($)*	*Average annual GDP growth (1985-92)*	*Unemployment (%)*
Albania	28,748	3.4	1,163	340	+0.4	18
Bosnia-H.	51,129	4.3	10,667	2,454	+0.3	n.a.
Bulgaria	110,994	8.5	9,812	1,160	-1.3	23
Croatia	56,538	4.7	26,300	5,600	-1.1	19
Greece	131,957	10.4	76,679	7,390	+1.7	8
Hungary	93,033	10.3	30,894	3,000	+2.5	11
Macedonia[1]	25,713	2.1	1,709	780	+1.0	27
Romania	237,500	22.7	24,810	1,090	-5.5	15
Slovenia	20,256	2.0	12,744	6,330	-4.4	12
Turkey[2]	779,452	61.2	114,234	1,950	+6.0	8
Yugoslavia[3]	102,173	10.5	31,867	3,093	n.a	23
UK	*244,110*	*58.4*	*1,024,025*	*17,770*	*+2.0*	*10*

Note that these figures give an approximate guide only and may be based on different years. By 1995, war had produced a catastrophic decline in living standards in the former Yugoslavia, with annual GDP per head in Bosnia down to $250.

1 Formally known by the UN as "The former Yugoslav Republic of Macedonia" (see note on page 17).

2 The European part of Turkey, with some 14 million people in the area which includes Istanbul and Edirne, has the biggest population in the Balkans, apart from Romania.

3 The 'rump' state of Yugoslavia, comprising Serbia and Montenegro.

Source: Britannica Yearbook 1995, European Bank for Reconstruction and Development and other sources

The profits of war

Black marketeers and criminals often prosper during wartime, especially when they are given arms and authority by political leaders – as the gangster Arkan was by the Serbs. Thus there are powerful vested interests in continuing the conflict. The majority of people, of course, would benefit from peace, stability and co-operation between nations.

One of the biggest problems facing the whole of the Balkans in the next decade will be how to transform economies dominated by corrupt public officials and organised crime into an honest and properly regulated business environment.

The mixture of Islamic and Christian architecture produced over the centuries a marvellous cultural heritage in the Balkans. In Bosnia and Croatia, much of this beauty has been destroyed in the last few years as Serbs, Croats and Muslims have busily wrecked each other's buildings.

Apart from the sacrilege involved, there is a huge economic price. Reconstruction will take many billions of dollars. This money will have to come from the international community – already stretched by the need to support economic and political reform in so many other parts of the post-communist world.

away. In Albania, for example, blood feuds between clans were prohibited and literacy raised from only 15% in 1944 to 92% by 1990.

Largely peasant communities were transformed into the beginnings of modern industrial society. In Yugoslavia, a system of 'self-management' was developed which helped to end social inequalities but ultimately led to gross inefficiencies. The transfer of wealth from Slovenia and Croatia – the two most developed republics – to the poorer regions caused great resentment. The need to keep each ethnic group happy led to compromises, duplication of infrastructure and disruptive changes of policy.

Yet in 1990 Yugoslavia was the most advanced Balkan economy – aside from Greece which had the advantage of Western support and EU membership to bring it into the modern era. Romania, its oil wealth squandered on grandiose projects, remained in poverty, as did Bulgaria and Albania.

Now all three of these countries are struggling to enter the world of free markets. All three have great potential yet presently display the turmoil and crime waves which are accompanying post-communist reforms almost everywhere.

Romania's economy seems to be stabilising and foreign investors (e.g., Daewoo, Coca-Cola and Shell) are beginning to show more interest. The new private sector already accounts for a third of GDP, but 90% of industry is still in government hands. Albania, hoping to become the 'Taiwan' of the Balkans, now welcomes foreign investment and is encouraging development of its copper, chrome and oil deposits and its tourist potential. Fertile but resource-poor Bulgaria, grappling with high unemployment, environmental damage and political vacillation, has a former communist regime which is pressing ahead with reforms under the aegis of the EU and the IMF. In all these countries, governments have to cope with growing public impatience at the time taken to benefit from free market reforms. All have archaic industries which cannot compete on world markets but which employ most of the workforce. No wonder privatisation is slow to come.

Macedonia, heavily dependent on the Greek port of Thessaloniki for trade and oil, has suffered from the Greek blockade, lifted only in late 1995. New road, rail and energy links will encourage economic development. Macedonia should also be helped by its strategic position on trade routes and its tourist potential.

As a united country, Bosnia-Herzegovina seemed economically sustainable, with a good mixture of industries, agricultural and energy resources, and great tourist potential. Divided into two, the picture looks very different. Most of the best farmland and iron ore deposits are in the new Serb Republic, most of the industries and power stations are in the Muslim-Croat entity. Disruption has been massive, with over 60% of the population of 4.3 million having been driven from their homes by the war. Many of the country's intelligentsia have been killed or have left the country, leaving a shortage of management skills.

Large numbers of churches, mosques and historic buildings have been destroyed, as well as infrastructure such as bridges, houses, factories, and transport and telecommunication links. At least $6 billion is needed to finance the reconstruction of Bosnia alone, with the main burden falling on the EU.

In 1994, 'rump Yugoslavia' spent over 76% of its budget on military activities. Living standards plummeted. Hyperinflation – an annualised rate of over 300,000,000% by early 1994 – set new world records. The destructiveness of nationalism was starkly demonstrated.

Pressure Points

The former Yugoslavia is not the only place where tensions are high. Other frictions could ignite the dangerous tinderbox of the Balkans.

The interlocking mosaic of the Balkans

The prospect of a northern border lined with states friendly to Turkey alarms Greece, which sees Macedonia as a menacing, artificial creation. Others see the establishment of a multi-ethnic and democratic state in the central Balkans as a sign of hope for the future. Will the Balkan countries learn to build on each other's strengths? Or seek to exploit weaknesses?

Will the Balkan countries build on their potential for economic development and tourism? Or will such tranquil scenes be threatened by movements of refugees and 'economic migrants', arguments over maritime rights, inter-ethnic suspicion and military confrontation?

Richard Buckley

Nationalism is a relatively recent phenomenon in the Balkans, essentially dating from the 19th century. Greece provides a vivid example. As the Ottoman Empire declined, the great powers encouraged the development of Greek national consciousness as a way to push back the frontiers of Turkish dominion. There was also the idea that, as the birthplace of democracy, Greece deserved special support from the international community.

Gradually the Greeks began to embrace the notion of the 'big idea' (*megalí idéa*) which would bring together in a single nation all those lands inhabited by Greeks. It proved a popular notion but was bad news for the many Turks, Albanians, Slavs, Jews and Bulgarians who also lived in these areas. As Greek nationalism grew, so the Greeks turned against non-Greeks.

The exchange of Greek and Turkish populations in the 1920s (from which about 100,000 Greeks in Istanbul were exempt) did not remove ethnic tensions between the two countries. But the main conflicts between Greece and Turkey, which are both members of Nato, are over Cyprus and territorial rights in the Aegean.

Oil prospecting began in the 1970s and there appear to be considerable offshore reserves. Application of the 12-mile limit to all its islands would give Greece a virtual monopoly of oil production in the Aegean, but bring it into conflict with Turkish claims to 12-mile limits extending from the Turkish coast. Air traffic rights pose similar problems. Even so, there are growing business links between Greece and Turkey, which can be expected to strengthen with the EU's Customs Union with Turkey, effective from January 1996. Both countries have far more to gain from co-operation than conflict. It seems likely that the Greek government will take a less nationalistic tone following the end of the Papandreou era, and this should benefit peace and prosperity throughout the region.

Greece's relations with Albania are also sensitive, with about 75,000 ethnic Greeks living in the northern Epirus region of southern Albania. (Greek nationalist claims of 400,000 are clearly exaggerated.) At least 150,000 Albanians live in Greece, many of them unemployed. Ethnic tensions, which had died down after the Balkan upheavals of the early 20th century, could return if government action inflames them.

There are about six million Albanians in the Balkans, half of them living outside Albania (mainly in Kosovo and Macedonia). How these Albanian minorities can be safeguarded, without raising the question of realigning borders, is one of the most important and dangerous issues in the Balkans – especially in view of the high birth rate among Albanians.

Austria-Hungary and Italy encouraged the creation of an independent Albanian state partly to block Serbia's advance to the sea (which was achieved anyway when Montenegro joined Yugoslavia in 1919). If Montenegro now presses its claims to independence, Serbia might feel that its strategic interests could be threatened. Here is another issue that will need careful and moderate diplomacy if a 'military solution' is to be avoided.

Nationalism as a route to political power

The fomenting of nationalist feelings to gain power has been a common approach of politicians, though it often ends in disaster. Once established, authoritarian regimes control the media and may stifle the voices of moderation. Can long-term stability in the Balkans be achieved without democracy, press freedom and solid guarantees for human rights?

Wedged between Serbia and Montenegro is an area known as the Sandzak.* Muslims make up over 60% of its population of about 440,000. When ethnic cleansing spread in 1992, some 70,000 Muslims fled from Sandzak, which Serbs fear could join up with Gorazde and Sarajevo to form a Muslim entity. The Serbian portion of the Sandzak has come under severe police repression. Lack of Muslim rights and economic opportunities in the Sandzak provide another running sore.

In Bosnia, the behaviour of some Croats has evoked memories of wartime fascism. Such associations have not been helped by the choice of *kuna* for the name of Croatia's new currency (the *kuna* was used by the Pavelic regime in 1941-45). In some areas, the arrogance of Croat police towards the Muslim population, supposedly fellow-citizens in the new country, remains disturbing. The release of the indicted war criminal Ivica Rajic by a Croatian court in Mostar has outraged international officials, as does the continuation of black market racketeering and the failure to arrest Dario Kordic, another Croatian wanted for alleged war crimes.

Transylvania was part of Hungary for centuries and was transferred to Romania after World War I when Hungary lost two-thirds of its territory. Many of the people who live in modern Transylvania are of Hungarian ethnic origin. There is little public pressure for a return of Transylvania to Hungary but there is concern that the 1.7 million ethnic Hungarians in Romania are treated fairly. Similarly, there is concern over the insensitive attitude of the Slovak government to its Hungarian minority.

In Romania, where the former communist Ion Iliescu is still president, anti-Hungarian feelings have been allowed to gather strength. In the Transylvanian capital of Cluj, the strongly nationalist mayor, Gheorghe Funar, argues that concessions to Hungarians could lead to demands for an autonomous province. The official distribution of a new book, which accuses Hungarians of atrocities during the overthrow of Ceauçescu in 1989, shows how strong the nationalist elements in the government have become. Such attitudes throw into doubt Romania's commitment to democracy and human rights.

In short, the forces of nationalism still present the Balkans with serious dangers. Controlling them will require great political skills – and economic improvement.

The problem of Macedonia

When in 1991 the newly independent state of Macedonia (because of Greek sensitivity over the name, it is officially and awkwardly known as FYROM, "The former Yugoslav Republic of Macedonia") decided to use the Star of Vergina on its flag, the Greeks were outraged and alarmed. The Star of Vergina was a symbol used on the tomb of King Philip II of Macedon, father of Alexander the Great, arguably the most famous 'Greek' in history (though he was actually a Macedonian who adopted Greek language and culture). Slavs arrived in Macedonia in the 6th and 7th centuries. Along with others such as Bulgars, Greeks and Albanians, they have been there ever since. That modern FYROM, a mainly Slav country, should use the Star of Vergina on its flag struck the Greeks as theft of someone else's national symbol.

In the end, FYROM bowed to the pressure and adopted a less controversial emblem. Following this 'climbdown', extremists tried to assassinate FYROM President Gligorov in October 1995. Fortunately, the President, who has generally played a moderating role in Macedonian politics, seems to have recovered from his wounds, though at 78, he cannot be expected to continue for many more years. His replacement by a more nationalistic politician would be a cause of great concern. Meanwhile, the problem of the name remains, with Greece adamant that "Macedonia" is unacceptable. Alternatives such as Nova Macedonia, Slavmacedonia, the Vardar Republic, the Central Balkan Republic, Dardania and the Skopje Republic (Greece's name for the new state) have been proposed, but no agreement is yet in sight. Macedonia is also the name of Greece's northern province, an area which before World War I was populated largely by Slavs, Turks and Bulgarians but which has been associated with Greece since ancient times.

The EU recognised FYROM in April 1993 but Greece withheld recognition and trading links until September 1995 (following agreement on a new flag). FYROM joined Nato's Partnership for Peace programme in November 1995 and was recently admitted to both the Council of Europe and the Organisation for Security and Co-operation in Europe. Its stability and multi-ethnic credentials are of enormous importance in the region, bearing in mind its strategic position and the problem of the Kosovo Albanians and its own Albanian minority. In this context, the carving up of Bosnia along ethnic lines is very bad news for long-term regional stability.

The disputed flag of newly independent Macedonia, showing the Star of Vergina.

The new flag, agreed in 1995.

The Prospects for Peace

US intervention has stopped the war in Bosnia. But can an imposed settlement bring lasting peace? And what about all the other potential trouble spots?

The Dayton peace accord

In November 1995, in an extraordinary piece of diplomatic arm-twisting, the Americans persuaded the leaders of Serbia, Croatia and Bosnia to accept a new peace agreement, to be enforced by Nato.

The Dayton peace agreement, signed under great American pressure, provided for the partition of Bosnia along the lines shown below. The notion of a multi-ethnic state, which Bosnia has embodied for many centuries, has been abandoned. Opponents of the plan say that aggressive nationalism has been rewarded. Others argue that the accord provides the only chance for a gradual return to peace and sanity.

The events of the past few years have seen brutality and destruction on a huge scale in the Balkans. The viciousness of attacks of neighbour against neighbour makes it difficult to see how they can forgive and forget. Yet the aftermath of World War II shows how quickly new relationships between countries can develop. Who would have believed that France and Germany would patch up their differences so soon after 1945? Much depends on the attitude of the countries' leaders in persuading people to make a fresh start.

In this respect, there may be some hope for the future, though there should be no illusions about the motives of self-interest which come into play. Military setbacks and economic pressure have forced Serbia's President Milosevic to turn from warmonger to peacemaker, casting aside the more fanatical nationalism of the Bosnian Serbs in favour of a more pragmatic line. Croatia's President Tudjman seems unlikely to jeopardise his territorial and political gains by unnecessary intransigence in Bosnia. Bosnia's President Izetbegovic must be keenest of all to see a new spirit of co-operation in his shattered country.

The Croatian army, re-armed and re-organised into an effective fighting force, is now more than a match for the Serbs and the territorial integrity of Croatia seems assured. Krajina and even Eastern Slavonia have been returned to Croat rule, and half of Bosnia is effectively under Croat protection. The important rail link between Zagreb

Main points of the Dayton accord

- Bosnia-Herzegovina will continue within its present boundaries but will consist of two entities, the Federation of Bosnia and Herzegovina (the Muslim-Croat federation), which will control 51% of the country, and the Serb Republic (Republika Srpska) which will control 49%.
- The central government, based in the capital Sarajevo, will be responsible for foreign policy, trade, customs and immigration, monetary policy, international law enforcement, communications, transportation and air traffic control. There will be a three-person executive presidency with two elected members from the Federation and one from the Serb Republic. The bi-cameral legislature will comprise delegates from both entities. There will also be a constitutional court and a central bank.
- Free and fair elections (supervised by the OSCE) will be held within six to nine months. Refugees will be able to vote in their original place of residence.
- Nato's peace implementation force (Ifor) will have freedom of movement throughout the country and will be able to use force to get its way (UN forces, operating between 1992 and 1995, had neither of these powers)
- Both parties (plus Serbia and Croatia) must co-operate fully with international investigation and prosecution of war crimes. The constitution will guarantee the "highest levels" of human rights for all citizens.
- Trade sanctions on Serbia will be lifted, as will be the arms embargo on Bosnia.

What hope for Bosnia?

Bosnia has been split into two halves along ethnic lines. Cynics argue that this solution has given Serbia and Croatia most of what they wanted.

Meanwhile, resentment over the West's failure to stop the bloodshed and its insistence on painful economic reforms in the Balkan states carry the danger of a backlash against the notions of democracy and free markets.

and Split is now entirely under Croat control. Croatia looks to be emerging as a strong nation, with good economic prospects. If any state has gained from the war it is Croatia. Yet the leadership of Franjo Tudjman is authoritarian and intolerant, providing an obstacle to Croatia's integration into the EU and embarrassing Germany, Croatia's main EU ally.

Slovenia, which started the break-up of Yugoslavia, managed its transition to independence with remarkably little bloodshed. It seems well on the way to becoming a prosperous country and a member of the European Union. Ethnically homogeneous (about 90% of inhabitants are Slovenes), Slovenia's cultural instincts seem closer to Western Europe than to the Slav east.

In other parts of the Balkans, there are some encouraging signs. A new administration in Athens should improve relations between Greece and its neighbours. New road and rail links and oil and gas pipelines should help to bond the Balkan countries into closer economic and therefore political ties. EU pressure and the desire of Balkan states to be admitted as full members of the international community should serve to encourage moderation and respect for human rights.

But there are still many pitfalls on the way to peace and prosperity in the Balkans. The Dayton peace plan was imposed from the outside rather than willingly agreed by the parties directly concerned. Moreover the Nato plan to withdraw after one year may encourage nationalists to defer rather than abandon their plans. Unless Croatia's parastate Herceg-Bosna is completely dismantled, it is hard to see Muslims trusting in President Tudjman's good faith. Equally, it is difficult to see Serbs and Croats in Bosnia cheerfully co-operating in the building of a new multi-ethnic state.

Nato's mission, known as Joint Endeavour, is to keep the warring factions apart. Lieutenant-General Sir Michael Walker, the Briton who heads Nato's IFOR troops, has day-to-day command of a force of some 60,000 troops from both Nato and non-Nato countries. The operation is being run with three military zones under US, British and French leadership, the whole mission coming under the USA's Admiral Leighton Smith.

Nato's task, difficult enough in itself, is straightforward compared with the job of Carl Bildt, the EU envoy who is the international 'High Representative' charged with the business of integrating Bosnia's civil administration. While Nato has a clear mandate and a well-equipped force to carry it out, the High Representative has had to struggle with inadequate funding and uncertain authority.

Yet building a lasting peace in the Balkans will depend crucially on what happens in Bosnia. If ethnic cleansing becomes accepted as a policy option, the Balkan future will be grim indeed.

Kosovo and the Albanian question

One of the most dangerous trouble spots in the Balkans is centred on Kosovo, which lost its autonomous status within Yugoslavia in 1989 and is now under repressive Serb control. Some 80-90% of Kosovo's population of 2 million is of Albanian ethnic origin. However, Serbs regard Kosovo as their historical heartland, having moved into the area in the 6th century. By the 14th century, a substantial Serbian empire had been created under Stefan Dusan, with the patriarchate of the Serbian Orthodox church established in Pec. However, many Serbs left the area after the all-conquering Turkish army inflicted heavy losses on the Serbs at the Battle of Kosovo Polje in 1389. Most remaining Serbs were killed or driven out by the Ottoman Turks after Serb uprisings in the 17th century. Others moved north in response to Habsburg incentives to volunteer settlers. Albanians moved into depopulated 'Old Serbia' and have formed a majority in the area ever since. Many also live in neighbouring Macedonia.

Almost half of the six million Albanians in the Balkans live outside Albania. Fears that Kosovo might attach itself to Albania have driven much of the political manoeuvring of modern Yugoslavia. Tito gave Kosovo autonomy but the year after his death, police harshly repressed Albanian students protesting about poverty, lack of jobs and the 'colonial' attitudes of the Serbs. As Albanian demands increased, Serb nationalism began to grow in Yugoslavia, encouraged by a propagandist 'Memorandum' from the Serbian Academy of Sciences and Arts. The rise of Slobodan Milosevic dates from his visit to Kosovo in 1987, when he was seen on TV supporting a crowd of Serbs who were demonstrating against 'the growing Albanian threat'. Serbs argue that the much faster birth rate among Albanians is gradually swamping the Serb population. Serbs made up nearly a quarter of the population of Kosovo in 1948, but only 13% by 1981. If current population trends continue, Albanians will outnumber Serbs in the Balkan peninsula within a generation. Economic and educational disadvantages are mainly to blame for high birth rates among the Albanians, but such explanations get short shrift in nationalist circles.

Partition of Kosovo is advocated by some Serbs.The resource-rich north, which also contains Serb national monuments (such as ancient churches), would go to Serbia and the southern part to the Albanians as an autonomous area. Such a solution is unacceptable to Albanians.

Bibliography

Sources

The starting point for this issue was *Krisenregionen im südostlichen Europa: Aktuelle Landkarte 10/95*, Cornelsen Verlag, Berlin. Other sources included:

Daily News Bulletin, published by the Athens News Agency; "The Dilemmas of an Independent Macedonia", by Dr John B. Allcock, International Security Information Service, June 1994; *Encyclopaedia Britannica; The Economist; The Guardian; The Independent;* Human Rights Watch; *Journal of Area Studies*; "Managing Milosevic's Serbia", a discussion paper by Michael Robinson published in 1995 by The Royal Institute of International Affairs; Nato; *The Times; War Report*, the bulletin of the Institute for War and Peace Reporting (an independent conflict-monitoring and media-support charity based in London); United Nations; *Wounded Eagle: Albania's fight for survival,* by Marko Milivojevic, published by the Institute for European Defence and Strategic Studies, 1992; *The World Today.*

Books and other publications

Remaking the Balkans by Christopher Cviic, The Royal Institute of International Affairs, Revised edition 1995
(136 pages; ISBN 1-85567-295-2)

This analysis of Balkan affairs argues that internal pressures rather than international power politics is the main reason behind the upheavals of recent years. The author examines the role of communism in the Balkans, its tendency to sanitise past history (and thus allow resentments to fester beneath the surface), its failure to deliver on its economic promises – despite a wealth of natural resources – and the continuation of former communists in power in most Balkan countries. The book also discusses the rise of nationalism after the death of Tito (who was part Croat, part Slovene); the disintegration of Yugoslavia and the outbreak of inter-ethnic war; and the current relationships between Balkan states – concluding with the thought that economic self-interest could be the key to avoiding further conflict in the region.

Balkan Tragedy: *Chaos and dissolution after the Cold War,* by Susan L. Woodward,The Brookings Institution, 1995
(536 pages; ISBN 0-8157-9513-0; $18.95)

The author argues that "the Yugoslav conflict is inseparable from international change and interdependence, and it is not confined to the Balkans but is part of a more widespread phenomenon of political disintegration...This conflict is not a result of historical animosities and it is not a return to the pre-communist past; it is the result of the politics of transforming a socialist society to a market economy and democracy... A critical element was economic decline, caused largely by a programme intended to resolve a foreign debt crisis. More than a decade of austerity and declining living standards corroded the social fabric and the rights and securities that individuals and families had come to rely on." The West's failure to understand what was happening in the former Yugoslavia and its misdirected intervention only served to exacerbate the conflict.

Yugoslavia's Bloody Collapse: *Causes, course and consequences*, by Christopher Bennett, Hurst & Company, 1995
(272 pages; ISBN 1-85065-232-5; £9.95)

Described by the leading Eastern Europe historian Richard Crampton as "a concise, intelligent, sensible and sensitive short account", this book stresses that Yugoslavia's disintegration was not a product of centuries of strife but of a calculated attempt by a "handful of people" to forge a Greater Serbia. The author lays most of the blame for the Yugoslav tragedy on Slobodan Milosevic, who won control of the Serbian Communist party in 1987 and immediately turned from the Titoist policy of Yugoslavian 'brotherhood and unity' to a virulent programme of Serbian nationalism. A deliberately orchestrated press campaign to stir up fear and hatred of non-Serbs created a war climate in Serbia long before hostilities broke out. Although Bosnia was clearly an innocent victim when first engulfed by war, the international community, judging that no major strategic interests were at stake, cynically refused to get involved, clearly showing that "ethical considerations play no part in the foreign policies of the great powers".

Who Are the Macedonians? by Hugh Poulton, Hurst & Company, 1995
(218 pages; ISBN 1-85065-238-4; £12.50)

This detailed survey of the history of Macedonia from antiquity to the present covers the emergence of nationalism in the Balkans, the disintegration of the Ottoman Empire, the partitioning of Macedonia between Greece, Serbia and Bulgaria, the impact of World Wars I and II, and the Greek civil war. Later chapters examine how Tito fostered a separate Macedonian consciousness, using language and religion as building blocks. Current political issues are discussed, including the problem of the Albanian minority and Macedonia's relationship with neighbouring states.

Bosnia and Herzegovina: *A tradition betrayed*, by Robert J. Donia and John V. A. Fine. Jr., Hurst & Company, 1994
(318 pages; ISBN 1-85065-211-2; £9.50)

Pointing out that the Bosnian cabinet in 1993 contained nine Muslims, six Serbs and five Croats, the authors emphasise Bosnia's tradition of tolerance and co-existence going back many centuries. The history of Bosnia is surveyed from the Middle Ages, through Ottoman and Habsburg rule, to incorporation in 'royal' Yugoslavia after 1918, the upheavals of World War II, socialism in the Tito era and finally the descent into war – in the authors' view "an historical aberration" rather than a continuation of traditional inter-ethnic hostility. "Armed bullies and perpetrators of vicious ethnic cleansing" have been allowed to destroy a multi-ethnic society "that shared many of the values and beliefs that are central to Western democratic life".

The Death of Yugoslavia: by Laura Silber and Allan Little, Penguin Books, BBC Books, 1995
(400 pages; ISBN 0-14-024904-4; £6.99)

The book of a widely-praised BBC television series, broadcast in autumn 1995, which looks at the key characters and events in Yugoslavia's disintegration, exposing nationalist plans to divide the country by force of arms and grimly concluding that "in the post-Cold War world there is no collective security, no international will to protect the weak against the strong".

Other relevant publications include:

Atlas of Eastern Europe in the Twentieth Century, by Richard and Ben Crampton, Routledge, 1996; *Eastern Europe in the Twentieth Century,* by Richard Crampton, Routledge, 1994; *Minority Rights in Europe: The scope for a transnational regime,* edited by Hugh Miall, The Royal Institute of International Affairs, Pinter Publishers,1994; *Bosnia: A short history,* by Noel Malcolm, Macmillan, 1994; *Crimes without Punishment: Humanitarian action in former Yugoslavia,* by Michele Mercier, Pluto Press, 1995; *The Destruction of Yugoslavia: Tracking the break-up 1980-92,* by Branka Magas, Verso, 1993; *The Fall of Yugoslavia,* by Misha Glenny, Revised edition, Penguin Books, 1993; *The National Question in Yugoslavia: Origins, History, Politics,* by Ivo Banac, Cornell University Press, 1984.